A PROMISE OF LIVING

009

Published
April 2017

Title
A Promise of Living

Author
Allford Hall Monaghan Morris/
Simon Allford

Photography
Timothy Soar

Design
Graphic Thought Facility

Print
Pureprint Group

Specification
210 x 185mm, 108pp
Typeset in Franklin Gothic
Peyer Surbalin Jeansblau 135gsm
F-Color Glatt, 422 Naturbraun 120gsm
Fedrigoni Symbol Matt Plus White 170gsm
Fedrigoni Freelife Vellum White 120gsm

Copyright© 2017
Allford Hall Monaghan Morris Ltd,
trading as FifthMan

FifthMan
c/o Allford Hall Monaghan Morris
Morelands, 5-23 Old Street
London EC1V 9HL, UK

ISBN 978-0-9934378-2-3

Editor: Emma Keyte

FifthMan

A PROMISE OF LIVING
ALLFORD HALL MONAGHAN MORRIS & TIMOTHY SOAR

AHMMERICANA

In 2008, my wife Fiona and I hatched a plan to go on a delayed honeymoon. It was to be one of a series of unscripted drives across America. Oklahoma City was not on our list. The only plan was to land in Dallas, eat some fantasy-sized steaks, take in a rodeo and a big church service, and then drift west on or near Route 66 to end up in San Francisco. The song "Is this the way to Amarillo?" was popular at the time, and established another fix for New Year's Eve.

One evening, in the basement bar across the road from our Old Street office, a room empty except for a handful of staff and the cult characters from projected Japanese animations, I met Wade Scaramucci for an Asahi. The pretext was to discuss the design of the Angel Building but the conversation inevitably roamed, and finally settled on, our respective transatlantic love affairs. As a teenage Def Leppard fan, he had longed to visit Sheffield. Meanwhile, as a Sheffield Wednesday supporter, I was seduced by the American dream. So, at some point, his home town of Oklahoma City got added to our itinerary.

And so it was, in late December that we arrived at the Skirvin Hotel in Oklahoma City. Which, I was to discover, is Wade's town. Wade is a Southsider, which to most is the wrong side of the river. But his Ma, Avis, had helped reinvent Bricktown. She ran Nonna's, a restaurant which kick-started the regeneration of the city and had become the place to eat. She owned the Painted Door—a shop in the Skirvin where Fiona bought a dress. Her husband Phil, an engineer-inventor, and his brother, Jay, ran a valve factory (founded by his Italian immigrant father) which produced thousands of valves either for urgent business or to stockpile. As I discovered, Oklahoma is a boom and bust kind of town.

During this brief stay, I learned of the legend of the Sooners who jumped the gun in the 1889 land race. Of Deep Deuce, the jazz town. Of the Santa Fe railroad that cut the young city in half. Of the magnificent historic district of Heritage Hills with its palatial Prairie Houses.

And of the adjoining, but more modest, Mesta Park, leading onto the Citizens Bank Tower and the Gold Dome. The former is inspired by Frank Lloyd Wright—only with the louvres offering shading to the north—and the latter, Bucky Fuller. Both were built in the city's post-war golden age before the white flight to Nichols Hills left an empty Downtown dominated by car parks, and before IM Pei came up with a plan to banish tornadoes from Oklahoman life by demolishing what was left and building a city underground.

We took in a basketball game to see the Oklahoma Thunder (the recently imported NBA basketball team formerly named Seattle SuperSonics) continue their losing streak. But no one cared: relegation does not exist here in concept or reality. As is the way in Oklahoma, Wade knew someone who knew someone, and we ended up drinking with the team's owners. As an Englishman abroad, I engaged the cheerleaders in conversation. We drove around a good deal and said "hi" to a lot of people we did not then know. We ate at Nonna's and went to a few dive bars in Midtown and Automobile Alley. To us, Oklahoma City seemed empty, but that's what it's like in a city that is either freezing cold or oppressively hot. Everyone relies on the automobile and air conditioning. Which explains why the city founders, who had neither and little else, are still revered.

A few months later, back at our Japanese dive bar, Wade picked up on a late night Midtown bar conversation from the trip I could barely recall. It was 2009, London was rocky and Oklahoma was booming, so why not open an office there? Apparently, as Wade always notes, I suggested it.

Wade's family heritage had allowed him to get an Italian passport and escape his hometown nearly two decades before. He was to be the pioneer of project AHMMericana but he had no intention of being a settler (London had started off as his escape plan but had become his home). The plan was for him to fly into Will Rogers International Airport every six weeks (we always fly via somewhere else for, as far as anybody knows, the only international flights to OKC are from Mexico). I would fly out in support three or four times a year. The road trips had inspired a new adventure.

It was hard graft for Wade. He knew a few people, he met new people, and he found a supporter in Shannon Self. Shannon, a lawyer and man-about-town, made introductions to several of his acquaintances who owned parcels of land and old building stock. Our first building, always a milestone and only completed in 2014, was for Tarena Self, Shannon's sister. Tarena runs a hair salon, drives a hearse and bought the old bible bindery by the railways, magnificently named after its washed-out but still clearly visible painted slogan: "Jesus Saves".

It was fun for me as it was an adventure, and if you read—or watch—The Grapes of Wrath, you'll know Oklahomans are bodacious but hardy. They say little but will support fellow travellers. Especially those who show an interest in their city.

Larger projects followed. With Richard McKown and other investors (there are always interested locals just a few calls away) we built LEVEL. An entire city block of two hundred and twenty-four apartments for rent. We solved the challenge of accommodating one car per room by wrapping a car park with two courtyards and an inhabited wall. In true American style it offers the best of the new and old worlds. You get the European urban ideal of corner shops, front doors and a busy street life with the American dream of driving to your front door! Construction is in feet and inches, and is about exploiting the efficiency of concrete for cars and balloon-frame timber for people. Wind (if not tornadoes) and the need to modulate the form established the principle of the repetitive recessed balconies. Mosaic, located on a smaller plot, demanded a different organisation of cars and people, and a better render incorporating mica. OKSea, across the way from both, uses shipping containers to house a number of businesses including a corn dog bar (the treat at last year's State Fair was deep-fried butter!).

Over on the western side of town we built, for Chip Fudge, a new block for the Hart Building —a massively constructed two-storey warehouse on Film Row. Chip is, among many other things, a collector of warehouses, splendid vintage cars, motor bikes and debt. We gratefully moved our office into the Hart (from what were some unseemly metal containers more suitable for storing goods than accommodating people). We have since relocated to The Plow, formerly the home of the Rock Island Plow Company, a derelict listed warehouse with a magnificent timber frame. Again, Richard is involved, as are investors from previous projects.

In the last few years, until his untimely death, we worked with Aubrey McClendon and his wife Katie. We visited them in Bermuda where we designed them a new home. In Oklahoma City, the campus for their new business, American Energy LP, was to set a new benchmark for volume, light, air and amenity. Sadly only the first phase, the AELP Fitness Centre, was built. There Aubrey asked us to turn a glorious folly—a giant basement he had started building to store his fine wine collection—into a more publicly useful sports building and crèche. We are now building the first phase of a different campus, reinventing a series of found warehouses in Midtown for the Bob Moore Auto Group, having first developed an understanding with them when we built a prototype floating home on Lake Texoma. Cliff and Leslie Hudson have also become patrons, commissioning us to turn a single-floor office at level twenty-seven of an art deco Downtown skyscraper into a family home, and to build a new poolhouse in the gardens of their weekend escape on Grand Lake.

Every year since we began "breaking dirt" in Oklahoma we have invited another fellow traveller, Tim Soar, and his apprentice Tom to come with us for a week and make his own photographic record of what he sees. We show him around, and then when we go to work he does the same. At the end of the long day we eat deep-fried pickles and drink local beers. We give him little instruction and few words are exchanged. Which is how it should be in Oklahoma. This is his record of what he saw.

Simon Allford

Oklahoma City -'89
87337

BOOM

WB Skirvin didn't know architecture. He didn't really know anything about hotels either. But the oil wildcatter knew that if he wanted to make a splash as a newcomer in Oklahoma City, he had to hire the best architect to create a landmark worthy of his name. Solomon Andrew Layton was himself a relative newcomer, having arrived in Oklahoma City about the same time as Skirvin. Layton was 47 years old and thanks to Skirvin, he was set to become an icon in Oklahoma City's architectural community. The hotel they designed and built, fuelled by rounds of late night drinks, grew twice, from six to eight storeys and then from eight to ten. The men collaborated repeatedly on further expanding the hotel, adding a third wing and finally increasing the height to 13 storeys.

Skirvin was right. Layton went on to design the Oklahoma State Capitol, the second Oklahoma County Courthouse, was hailed as the state's most legendary architect upon his death and his name graces the state's top architectural award a century later. Like many of Oklahoma's early architects, Layton came from a fairly modest upbringing and saw the blank slate that was Oklahoma City as an opportunity to build great landmarks—often by winning favour with the city's new millionaires.

Layton was born to a family of carpenters and mechanics, making construction a natural interest for him as a youth. After graduating high school in Red Oak, Iowa, he took a job as superintendent of mine construction and then opened his own office in 1887. When the mining boom ended, he applied for architectural work at Southwestern University in Georgetown, Texas. He missed the 1889 Land Run that gave birth to Oklahoma City, but joined the opening of the Cherokee Outlet in 1893 and attracted attention for his design of the county courthouse in El Reno. Layton was in his early 40s when he arrived in Oklahoma City, at a time when work was just starting on its first real skyline. An economic depression during the 1890s had stunted the city's development, but that was changing with discoveries of oil and shrewd recruiting of railroads and commerce by city fathers.

For William Wells, it was a public project that initially drew him to Oklahoma City. Wells was an Iowa youth who, watching the construction work done by his grandfather, enrolled at the Chicago Art Institute, where he listed his local mailing address as Frank Lloyd Wright's architecture studio in Oak Park. In 1897, at age 19, Wells gave a hint of his ambition, writing to Architecture and Building Magazine asking, "What do you consider the two best textbooks to be studied by a student in an architect's office?" Specifically, Wells wanted textbooks addressing strength of materials, roofs and trusses, heating, ventilating and plumbing.

Wells considered starting his career in Omaha, but quickly turned to the Oklahoma Territory, where at age 26 he won the commission in 1904 to build the first Oklahoma County Courthouse. For his first major work, Wells went with a Romanesque approach to design, aimed at making it the focal point of the 14-year-old city. Wells may have been among the first, but not the last architect to see his vision compromised by the divided interests that had set the tone for uneven development from the first week in 1889 that the city was established. Some business and political interests pushed for the courthouse to front Main Street while others sought to have it front Grand Avenue (now Sheridan Avenue). The courthouse was a stunning structure extending up from the frontier skyline, with exterior walls constructed of Indiana limestone, interior floors finished with granite and the walls and stairways built with Vermont marble. The building, however, ended up fronting Dewey Avenue between the two streets, creating an awkward public view along a far less prominent street. The ornate entrance was often skipped by visitors who chose to enter from the less prominent side entrances facing Main Street and Grand Avenue.

New-found riches driving the emergence of the first real skyline didn't derive exclusively from discoveries of oil. After building the courthouse, Wells' next job was to design a new corporate headquarters for Pioneer Telephone. The company started out when Perry farmer John Noble, mercantile owner Eugene D Nims, and Santa Fe station agent Emery E Westervelt joined together to create a state-wide telephone system. Noble had the background for such ambition with electrical engineering training at the University of Kansas. He worked briefly at the Chicago Telephone Company before he homesteaded a farm near

Pawnee, Oklahoma. Noble later wrote that during those four years as a farmer, he felt isolated and concluded Oklahoma could not progress without a system of communication. He borrowed money and in 1897 he built a long-distance line from Pawnee to Perry at a cost of $2,200. After joining with Nims and Westervelt, the company prevailed while other start-ups faltered. They bought up territories and controlled more than 25 exchanges when in 1904 they took control of the Oklahoma City network.

Three years later, it was time to build a grand headquarters for Pioneer Telephone, which had moved its operations to several leased spaces in Oklahoma City. They hired Wells as he was adapting to a style taught by another of his mentors, Chicago architect Louis Sullivan. The pioneer in skyscraper design taught Wells new techniques for building multi-storey structures—training that was noted by executives at Pioneer Telephone as they looked for an architect to design a new home to consolidate their 150-employee operation. The Pioneer Building was the first multi-storey building built in Oklahoma City with a steel frame, an architectural innovation that would quickly transform the entire skyline. The building, completed in 1907, featured cut-stone columns, plate-glass windows, and two ornately engraved entries. Columns on the fifth floor were etched with a terracotta ornament in a floral pattern. Interior corridors were finished with Georgian marble with wainscoting, while the main entrance was built with Italian marble.

Wells also encountered a dynamic that would plague Oklahoma City for decades—the incomplete vision. Charles Colcord was a frontier cattleman and lawman who arrived during the 1889 Land Run and later set up an investment company with holdings extending into oil. Joined by Bob Galbreath, Colcord purchased lots at the northwest corner of Grand and Robinson Avenues in 1904. The properties consisted of prefabricated two-storey wood frame structures first shipped in by rail from Wisconsin and erected by city father Henry Overholser shortly after the Land Run. Overholser had invested in properties throughout the city, but was known to be struggling with debt. Galbreath wanted to build a hotel on the corner, while Colcord believed a hotel would not be profitable. Colcord bought out his partner's interest and then hired Wells, and tasked him with creating the grandest building yet for Oklahoma City. Colcord and Wells then travelled to San Francisco, Atlanta, Kansas City, St. Louis, Cincinnati and Chicago. "This was to be the first big building in Oklahoma City," Colcord later wrote. "I was anxious not to make any mistakes."

The 1906 earthquake that devastated San Francisco drew an immediate visit by Colcord, who discovered only 11 buildings still standing. Colcord observed they were all built from reinforced concrete, whereas the ones built with steel frames were taken down by the extreme heat of the flames. Colcord immediately worked with Wells to change their plans from steel to concrete. Though never confirmed by Wells, word spread around town that all of the plans were reviewed by Sullivan, who was at this point considered one of the country's top architects.

The Colcord Building was very much a reflection of Sullivan's influence. Marble columns, floors and walls were built inside to exude grandeur and permanence. Terracotta mouldings framed the ceilings. Modern conveniences included restrooms and decorative water fountains on each floor. Even the elevator doors and mailbox were finished with richly engraved nickel and bronze. The 12-storey building opened to rave reviews, with the Oklahoma City Chamber using the top floor penthouse to show off views of the growing skyline.

Wells' career in Oklahoma City was coming to an end as Layton was rising up to take his place as the city's premier architect. Wells did just three more projects in Oklahoma City, and in 1916 he left for Spokane, Washington. Oklahoma City architecture continued to evolve as oilmen colluded with architects to transform a prairie town into a major metropolis. But with the oil bust in the 1980s, some of the city's most talented architects moved away, leaving older firms left to survive with what few jobs were left.

Out of that economic depression, however, arose a new crop of architects and patrons eager to make their ambitious ideas a reality. The first big surge started with a decision by voters to pass a five-year, one-cent sales tax to fund public projects throughout the city. Arts patrons bickered over whether to gut and rebuild the auditorium inside the historic

1937 Art Deco Civic Center Music Hall or whether to build a new home for the arts in northwest Oklahoma City. The Civic Center crowd won the debate, and the historic shell now houses a modern performing arts venue that features a colourful set of balcony suites and a three-storey high lobby atrium.

Billionaire Aubrey McClendon, meanwhile, followed in the steps of WB Skirvin. No ambition was too great as he took an initial vision of a humble log cabin style boathouse and commissioned architects to kick off development along the Oklahoma River. McClendon was pitched a $300,000 plan that he rejected and replaced with a $3.5 million landmark. He led the fundraising for the Chesapeake Boathouse, got his employees involved in the new rowing programmes, and continued to support development of a masterplan for the river that today includes three widely acclaimed boathouses, a finish line tower, a zip-line, slides, bungee jump and ropes course super structure, a river rapids course and play areas for children.

A younger generation of developers, meanwhile, are transforming long neglected historic buildings and bringing them back to life. Pivot Project developers Ben Sellers, David Wanzer and Jonathan Dodson were all working separately when their vision for the urban core brought them together to work on bringing life to properties including the Tower Theater, Main Street Arcade, and the Sunshine Laundry.

The transformation of Oklahoma City continues, no longer stunted by downturns in the energy industry. New towers continue to arise as the city continues to invest in improvements that include a new convention centre, urban park and a streetcar system. Oklahoma City is a place where architects' grand visions have a shot at coming true thanks to a community of equally imaginative patrons, many of whom do not need to be plied with drinks to buy into the dream.

Steve Lackmeyer

1

3

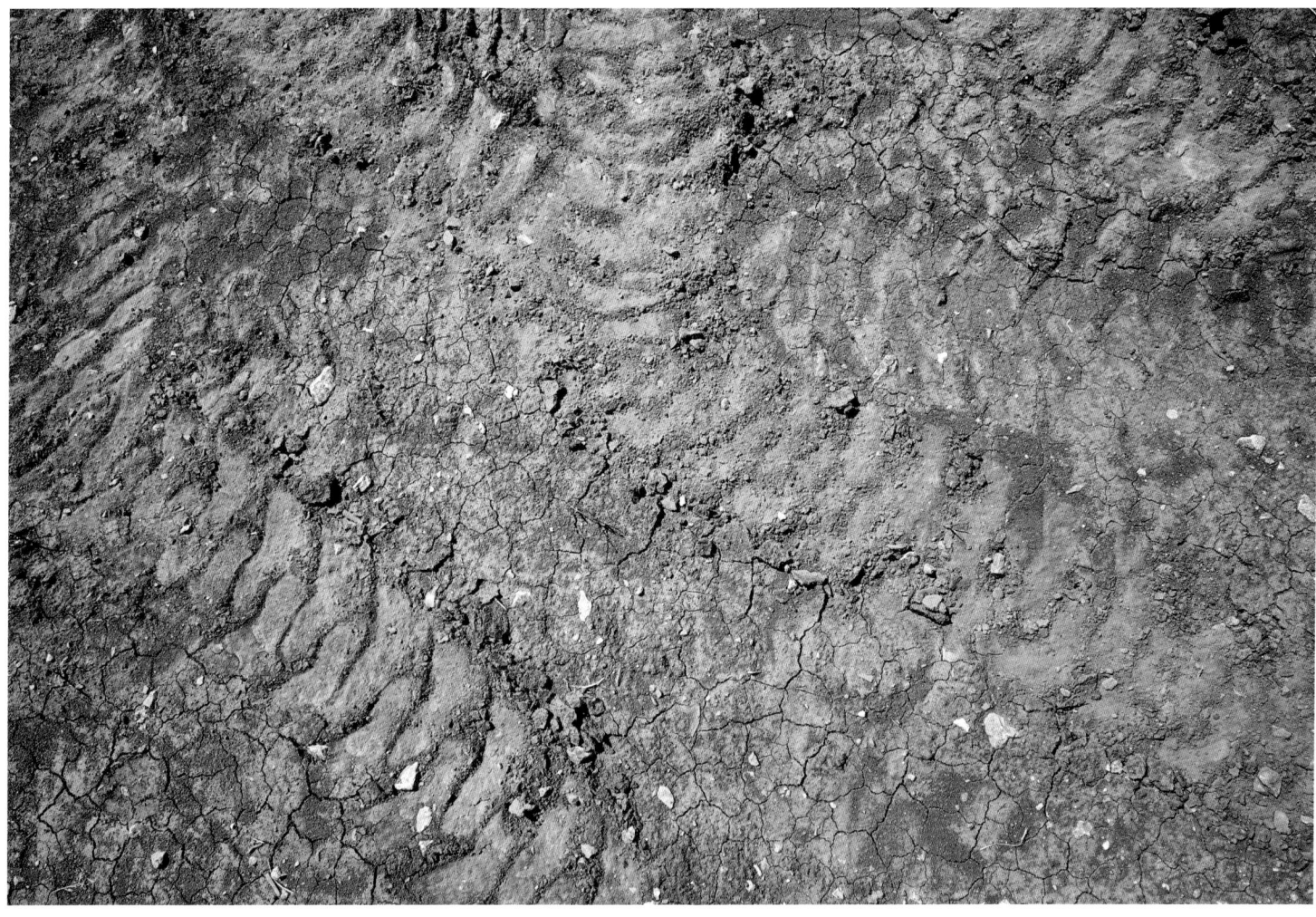

6

7

8

11

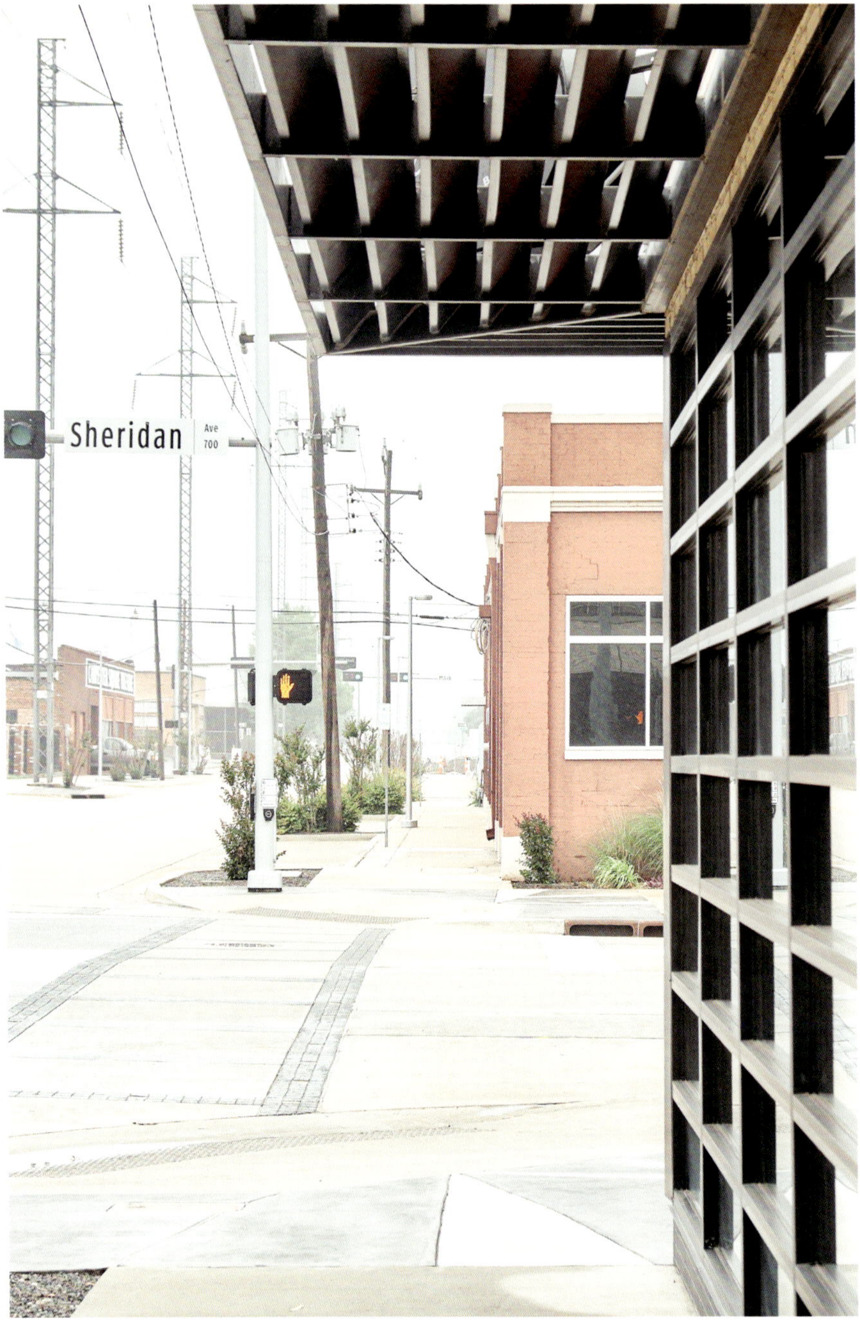

12–13

14–15

16

17

18

19

20

21

22

24

25

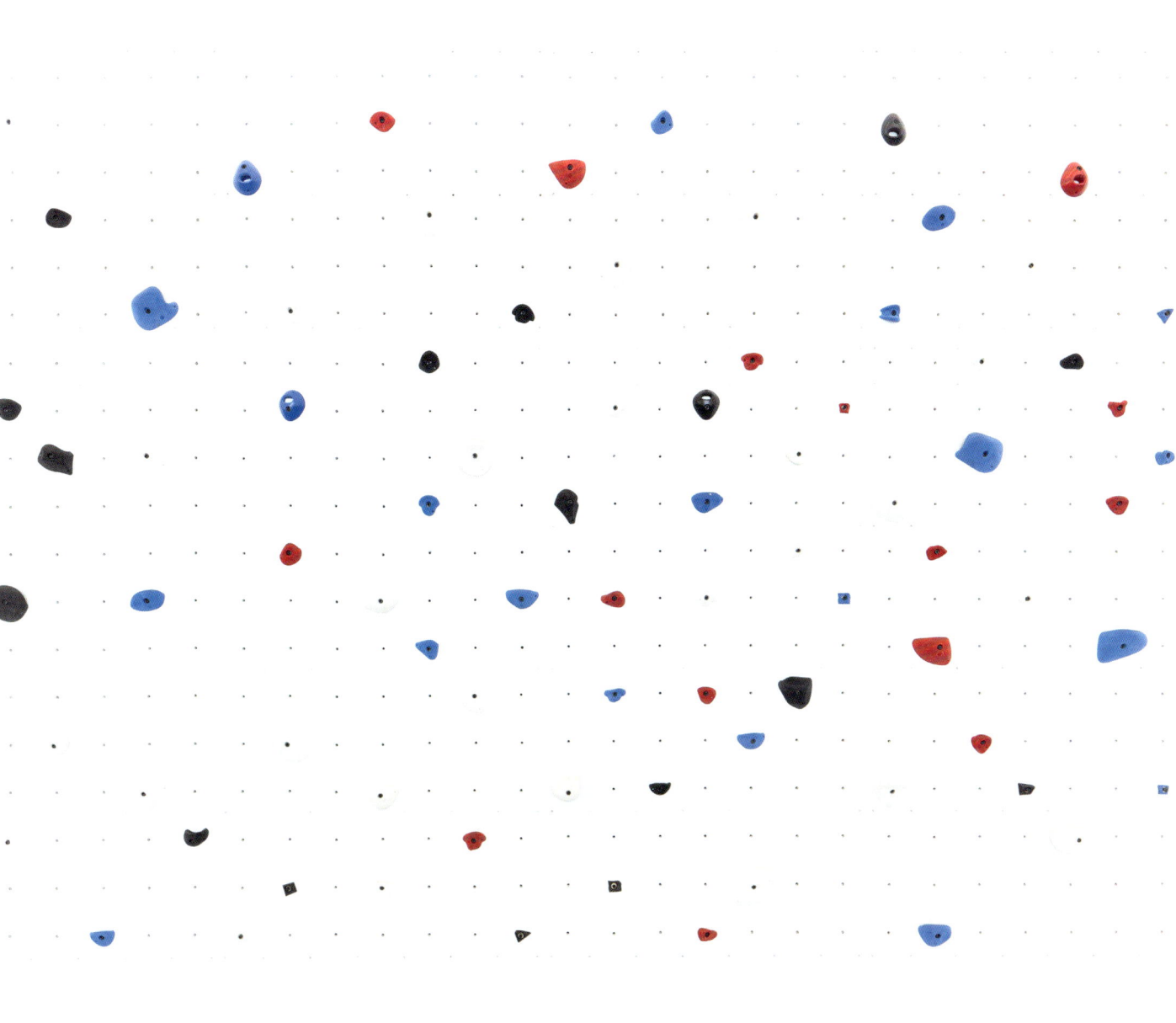

26

28

30

33

34

35

37

38–39

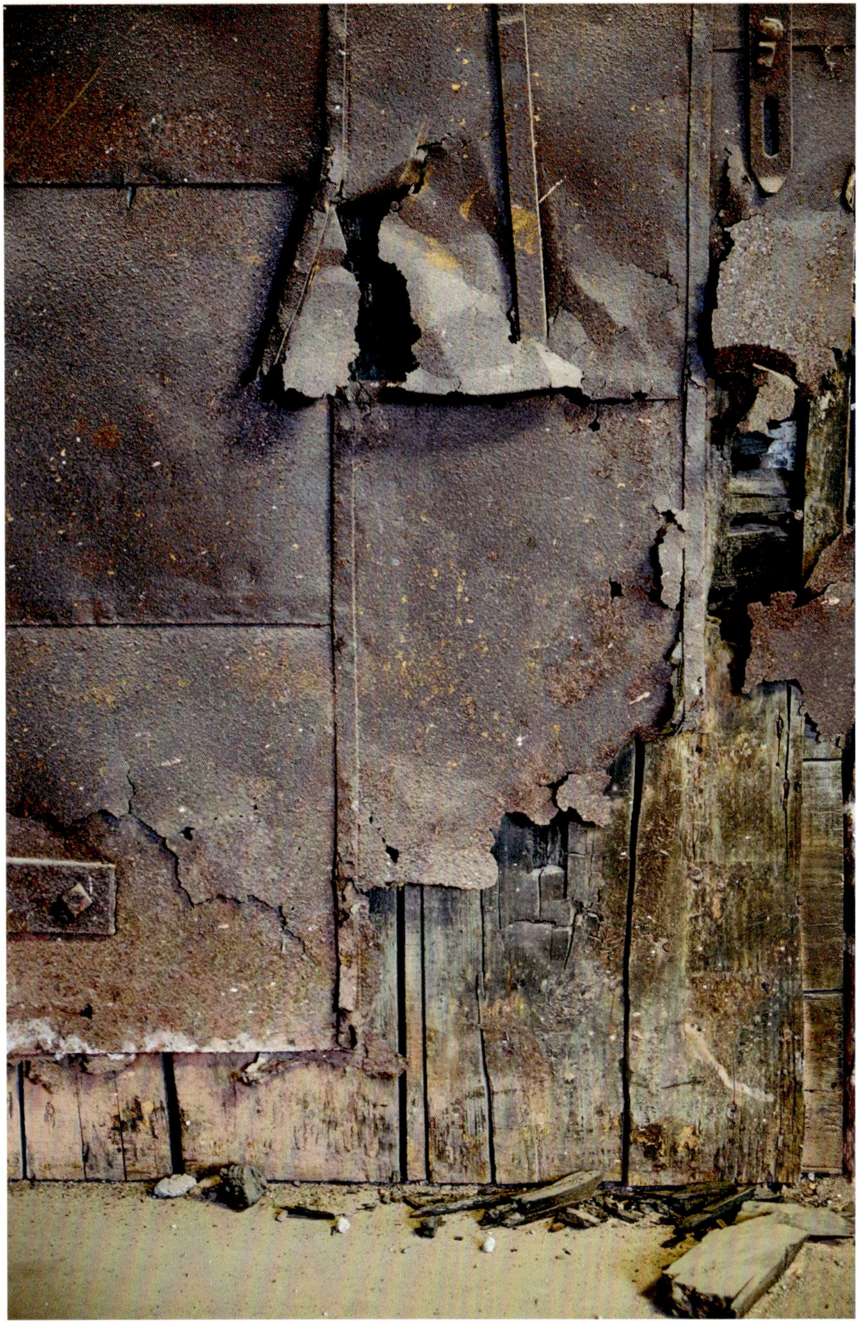

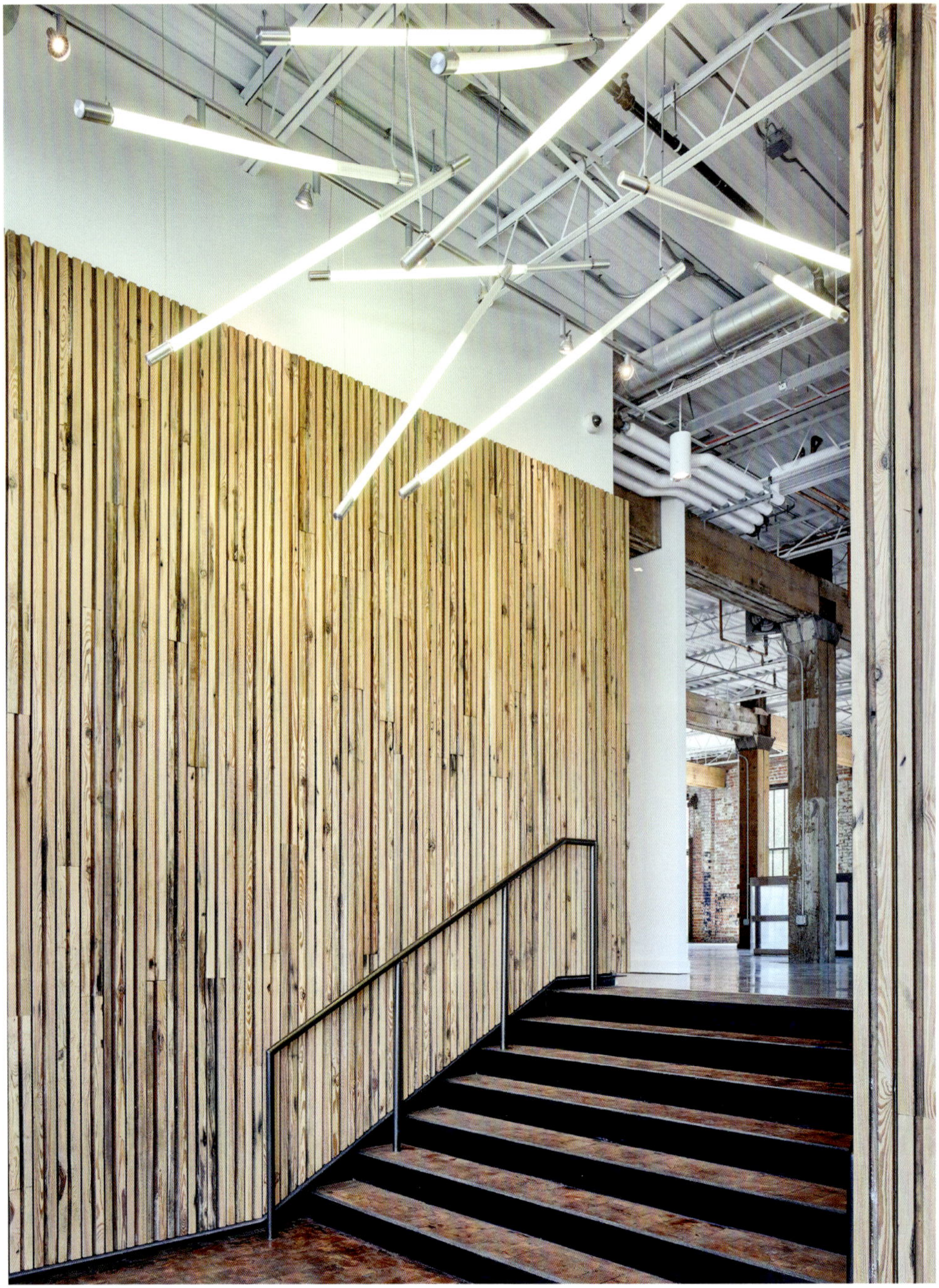

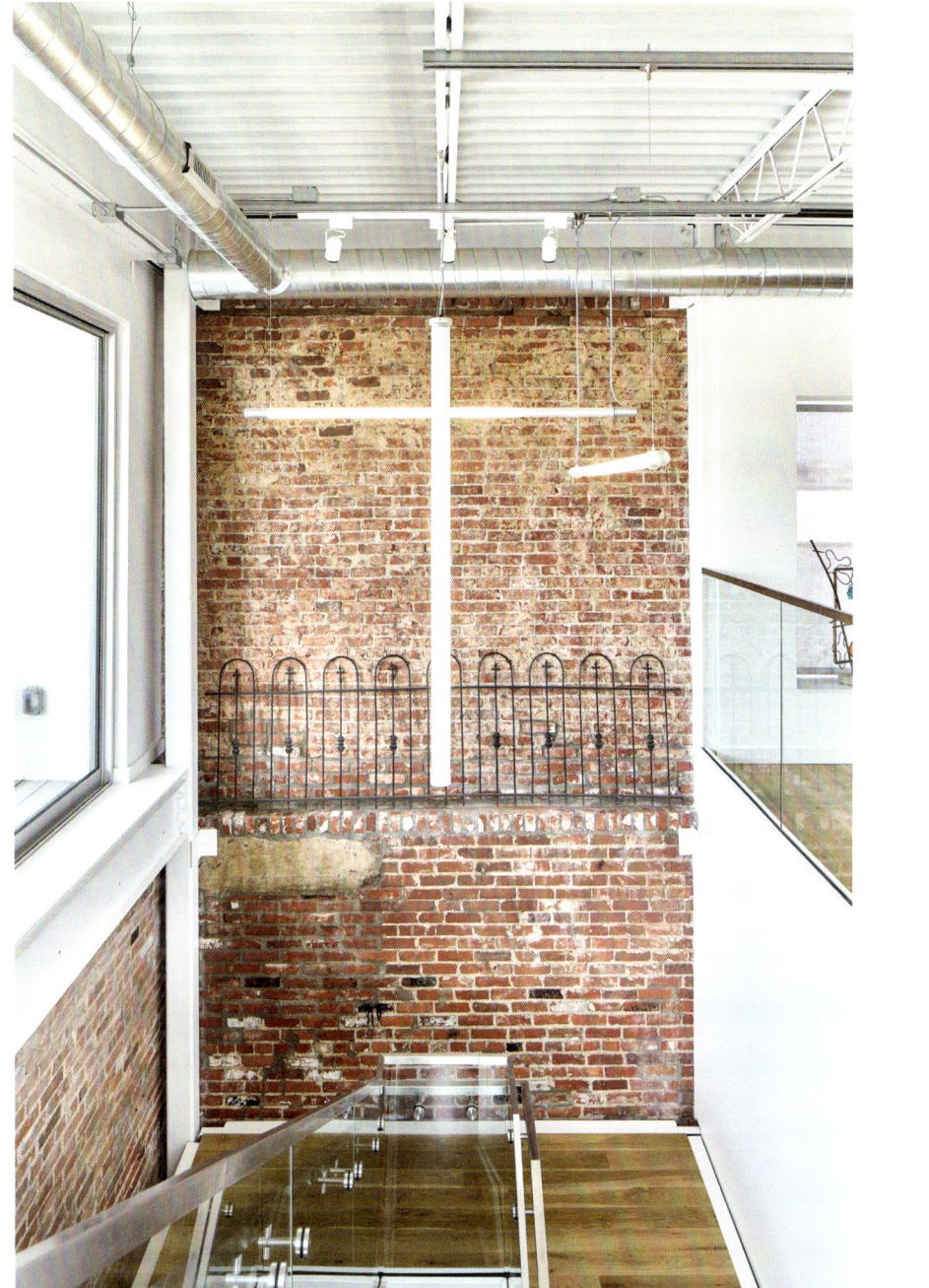

42

43

45

46

A PROMISE OF LIVING

Photography is a curious medium, somehow ill-equipped to be a truthful witness with so many conceits, feints, sleights of hand, and darkened shadows to misdirect and misinform. It is also a poor liar, too connected to the actual—each frame constructed as it is by the energy of reflected light from a real physical form. Post-production can manipulate or distort but can never provide the authenticity of that actual recording. We always know when we are being deceived, even if that knowing is manifest only as a fleeting sense. The balance of the photographer's judgement between deception and truth is the spirit in which the photograph is made.

In the twenty-first century, there are not many clients willing to commit the time, resource, capital and trust into a creative project as open-ended and as vulnerable to failure as that which has become A Promise of Living. Flying a photographer from London into uncertain weather and unfinished buildings is a gamble fraught with the possibility of barren days and empty contact sheets. But having taken that risk, something very special is coming into focus and that object, becoming clearer and brighter on every visit, is the spirit, soul and energy of Oklahoma.

One of the fascinating things attending this commission was the brief, which was a simple one: do your magic. Of course, there's quite a bit to the discipline of architectural photography which is less about magic than it is about due diligence—covering the bases, explaining form and illustrating context. There is a continuous dialogue between the needs of self-expressive art and an entirely selfless, clear, honest and unambiguous description. There is always a narrative, and in my case, mostly because of my temperament, the narrative is permanently skewed by the admiration and respect I have for my architects and what they achieve. So in my world, truth is an imagined thing, to do with heroic achievement, noble purpose, selfless dedication. Everything that we see, everything that is built, everything that has been achieved has been done by dint of a will: it has all been made to happen. Making photographs of buildings is very similar to making portraits of people.

You need to learn what they are about, what their backstory is, the problems they have overcome and the hope embedded in them for the future. The portrait must also be attended by a subtle sense of the best light, to reveal those aspects of character that seem to best represent the sitter. These are not always the most flattering, but if correctly done, are the most appealing. With honesty and clarity an affectionate relationship can produce photographs of joy, and delight; of shared discovery and the strange alchemy that occurs when you are working with your sitter, rather than despite them.

So this project, as it has progressed, has not just been about photographing an emerging architecture, it has been about learning a climate, a light, a way of being. Many new ideas have had to be incorporated into the photographic practice and many new things learnt. Oklahoma City is a place of enormous contrasts: the blinding brightness of the light on a summer day of 100 degrees or the enveloping fog when it's close to freezing. Even on the brightest day, the shadows on an Oklahoman street are bright, open, full of detail. There are none of the inky shadows and concealed portals that are a feature of European cities, configured as they are around narrow streets and canyons of clustered buildings. The gigantic sky, a canopy of saturated azure, returns light from every angle. Here, every building is an individual sculpture bathed in light. Having become familiar with the baking pavements and searing heat, returning in tornado season is to experience another city altogether. Rains now accumulate to form rivers where roads once were, mists form so thickly you can see the water droplets hanging in the air. The light is so soft and diffuse, you could be walking through a conjuror's dry ice. Buildings disappear and perspectives end in washes of featureless grey. In such extremes, it is as though the buildings are remade in every new day's light.

Oklahoma, then, is a city of drama and contrasts, only survived by ingenuity and grit. The drama and spectacle of the weather remind you that for the unlucky, or the poorly prepared, this place can strip away your skin or suck the air from your lungs. It's unforgiving and ruthless, constantly present. One of the great gifts of travel is being able to observe how we as a species meet and manage such challenges of climate and culture. There is something very specific in the character of an Oklahoman: optimism, ideas, persistence, the certain knowledge that within a community fellowship will be found and solutions will be discovered. There is also a grace, an acceptance that not every challenge will be overcome. To paraphrase Kipling, Oklahomans seem to meet triumph and disaster with a perfect symmetry of stoicism and humour.

A striking feature of our visits was how we were remembered in coffee shops, car hire desks, on the street, by the construction teams. Four brief visits over two years but we've clearly been remembered, perhaps like revisiting cowboys ahead of a herd of cattle or the itinerant oil men who have capped wells over the city. Everywhere we went we were met with genuine warmth and enthusiasm, offers to exploit the best viewpoints and requests to return. All spring from the deep well of community that is Oklahoma City. It's as though the covered wagon train, the shared campfire and the vital need to trust your neighbour still endure.

Oklahoma invented itself one day in 1889; from nothing it made itself the state's largest city and one of the largest cities by landmass in the USA. Photography has always been part of its culture and mythology. Photographers like "That Man Stone" arrived to document the birth of the city, armed with the latest panoramic camera technology. They assiduously photographed each new building and railhead, the characters and events that shaped the structure and personality of the city. An essential part of the Oklahoman idea of itself is that first land rush and an attachment to the notion of an open frontier, a clean sheet, a place to make and express. It seems there is an endless Oklahoman restlessness to build, to start afresh, to create opportunity. In a place that is constantly reinventing itself, photography becomes essential, not just as memory and record but as a totemic instrument evoking a spirit of newness and recent completion, as though the photograph kept alive that restless desire to be in flux. Photographs speak of that moment, just prior to occupation, or the day when the frame of the barn is raised and memories of the potential of the activity are refreshed, rather than the enduring solidity of the finished work. Oklahomans seem to need the reassurance that their open sky still meets an open frontier.

Timothy Soar

OklahomaCity,

Indian Territory.
1890.

One of the inspirations for this book was James Agee and Walker Evans' *Let Us Now Praise Famous Men*. Tim Soar describes the book, written by Agee with photographs by Evans, as "mad, expansive, beautiful, confusing, passionate and ambitious beyond reason".

Let Us Now is a documentary piece, the result of a commission from *Fortune* magazine to record the lives of sharecroppers in Alabama during the great economic depression of the 1930s. Where Evans' uncaptioned black-and-white photography is uncompromisingly straightforward, Agee's text (much of it reworked when *Fortune* refused to publish it) is cyclical and shambolic, moving from deadpan documentary to poetic fragments.

In its turn *Let Us Now* inspired Aaron Copland's opera *The Tender Land*, a coming-of-age tale which also documents the lives of people working the land during the depression years. The first act of the opera ends with a choral quintet, "The Promise of Living", in celebration of the harvest. Our book also celebrates the promise of living deep-rooted in the American landscape, the promise in our case being that out of the red dust, great cities—and architecture—can grow.

PLATES

Image credits

Oklahoma City, Indian Territory, 1889; nsf/Alamy
T M Fowler view of Oklahoma City, Indian Territory,
1890; The New York Public Library Digital Collections

All other images © Timothy Soar

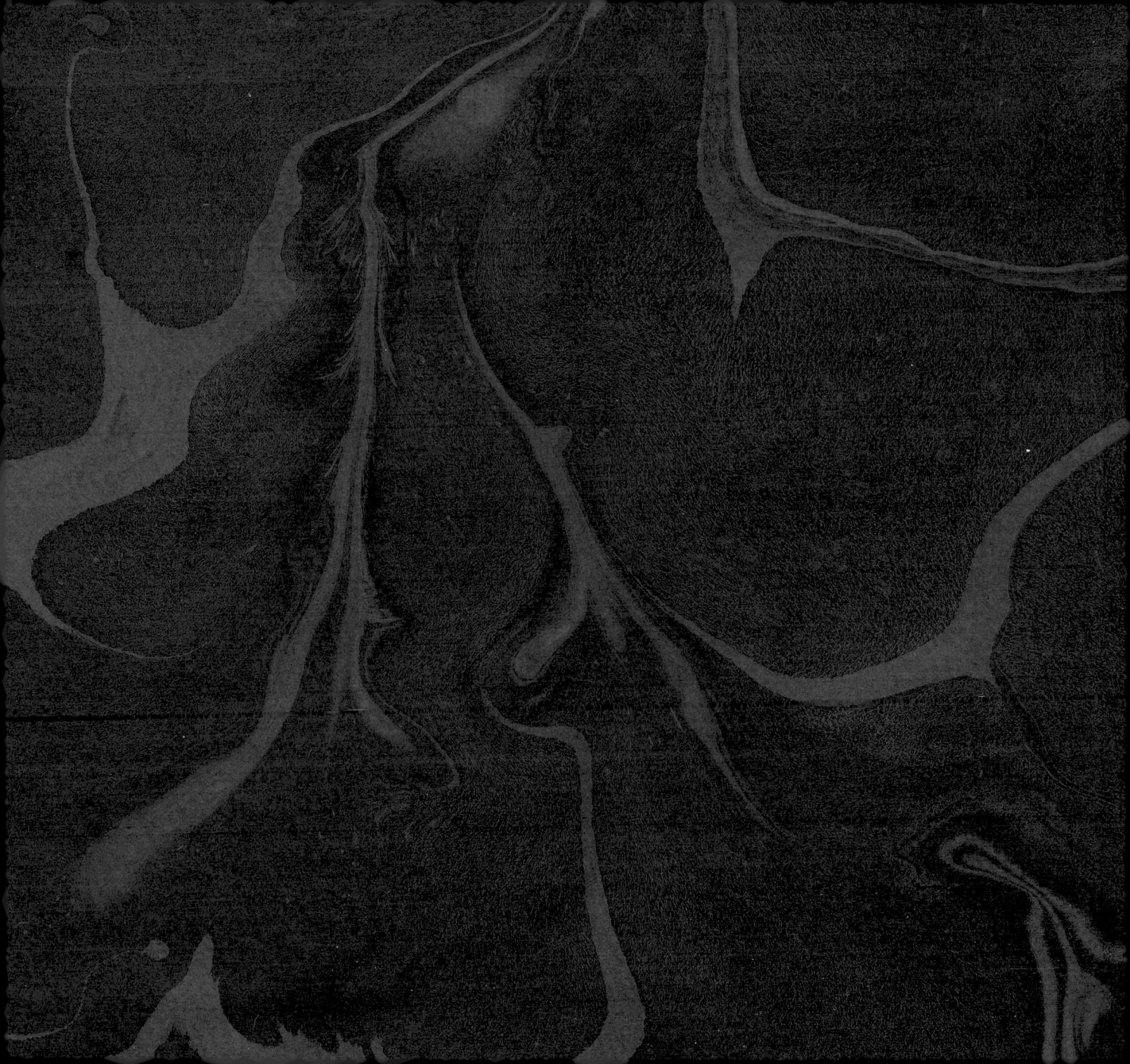